Date: 5/27/16

J 951.95 MUR
Murray, Julie,
South Korea /

SOUTH KOREA

EXPLORE THE COUNTRIES

Big Buddy Books

An Imprint of Abdo Publishing
abdopublishing.com

Julie Murray

abdopublishing.com

Published by Abdo Publishing, a division of ABDO, PO Box 398166, Minneapolis, Minnesota 55439.
Copyright © 2016 by Abdo Consulting Group, Inc. International copyrights reserved in all countries. No part
of this book may be reproduced in any form without written permission from the publisher. Big Buddy Books™
is a trademark and logo of Abdo Publishing.

Printed in the United States of America, North Mankato, Minnesota.
092015
012016

THIS BOOK CONTAINS
RECYCLED MATERIALS

Cover Photo: Shutterstock.com.
Interior Photos: ASSOCIATED PRESS (pp. 17, 19); Stephen Bay/Alamy (p. 35); Bloomberg/Getty Images (p.
  25); CRIS BOURONCLE/AFP/Getty Images (p. 31); © Mark Bowler/NPL/Minden Pictures (p. 23); Chung
  Sung-Jun/Getty Images (p. 11); Eye Ubiquitous/Getty Images (p. 35); Werner Forman/Getty Images (p. 13);
  David Harding/Alamy (p. 9); © iStockphoto.com (pp. 11, 15); JUNG YEON-JE/AFP/Getty Images (p. 15);
  Keystone-France/Getty Images (p. 17); Streeter Lecka/Getty Images (p. 33); Douglas MacDonald/Getty
  Images (p. 5); Pool/Getty Images (p. 19); SEUNG HWAN SHIN/Getty Images (p. 16); Shutterstock.com
  (pp. 19, 21, 27, 29, 34, 37, 38); White House Photo/Alamy (p. 35).

Coordinating Series Editor: Megan M. Gunderson
Editor: Katie Lajiness
Contributing Editor: Marcia Zappa
Graphic Design: Adam Craven

Country population and area figures taken from the CIA World Factbook.

Library of Congress Cataloging-in-Publication Data

Murray, Julie, 1969- author.
  South Korea / Julie Murray.
    pages cm. -- (Explore the countries)
  Includes index.
  ISBN 978-1-68078-070-3
1. Korea (South)--Juvenile literature. I. Title.
  DS907.4.M87 2016
  951.95--dc23
                                 2015028306

SOUTH KOREA

CONTENTS

Around the World 4

Passport to South Korea 6

Important Cities 8

South Korea in History 12

Timeline 16

An Important Symbol 18

Across the Land 20

Earning a Living 24

Life in South Korea 26

Famous Faces 30

Tour Book 34

A Great Country 36

South Korea Up Close 38

Important Words 39

Websites 39

Index 40

AROUND THE WORLD

Our world has many countries. Each country has beautiful land. It has its own rich history. And, the people have their own languages and ways of life.

South Korea is a country in Asia. What do you know about South Korea? Let's learn more about this place and its story!

Did You Know?

Korean is commonly spoken throughout the country. And, English is often taught in schools.

Mount Halla is South Korea's highest mountain at 6,398 feet (1,950 m). It is part of Hallasan National Park.

Passport to South Korea

South Korea shares a border with North Korea to the north. The Sea of Japan is to the east. The East China Sea is to the south. The Yellow Sea is to the west.

South Korea's total area is 38,502 square miles (99,720 sq km). More than 49 million people live there.

Did You Know?

South Korea is smaller than North Korea. But, South Korea has more people.

WHERE IN THE WORLD?

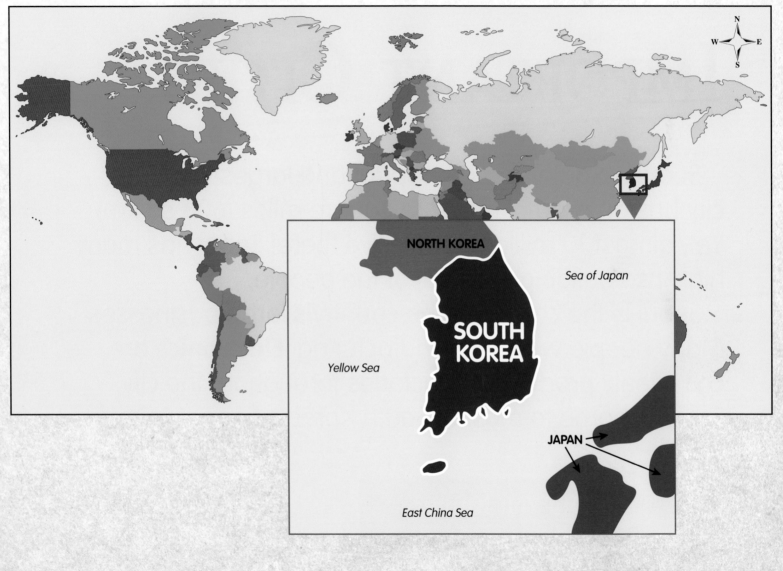

NORTH KOREA

Sea of Japan

SOUTH KOREA

Yellow Sea

JAPAN

East China Sea

Important Cities

Seoul is South Korea's **capital** and largest city. The city has an area of only 234 square miles (606 sq km). Yet, almost 10 million people live there! Seoul has many high-rise buildings to fit all of the people.

Seoul is the center for the country's large businesses. Many people work in manufacturing. **Electronics** are commonly produced in factories throughout the city. Seoul is home to most of South Korea's finance jobs.

Did You Know?

A stone wall was built around Seoul more than 600 years ago. It was built to guard the city from attackers. Today, some parts of the wall still remain.

SAY IT

Seoul
SOHL

SOUTH KOREA

Seoul

Inchon

Pusan

Seoul's Dongdaemun Design Plaza opened in 2014. The large building features a park, a museum, and many rooms for events.

Pusan is South Korea's second-largest city. It is home to more than 3.5 million people. It has many manufacturing jobs. The city's businesses include steel, ceramics, and shipbuilding.

Inchon is the country's third-largest city, with about 2.5 million people. This city makes goods such as steel, clothes, and glass. Some of South Korea's largest salt fields are close to this city.

SAY IT

Pusan
POO-sahn

Inchon
IHN-chuhn

The Pusan International Film Festival is one of the largest in South Korea. In 2014, 312 films from 79 countries were shown at the event.

International Film Festival
2-11 October, 2014

Inchon International Airport is one of the busiest in the world. The airport has comforts such as a golf course and an inside garden!

South Korea in History

The area that is now Korea was settled by people who traveled there from the north. Over time, farming improved with new ways of growing crops. Around 700 BC, travelers from China taught early Koreans new ways to grow rice.

In AD 1231, the Mongols **invaded** Korea. The Mongols came from what is now Mongolia and northern China. The Koreans did not easily give up their territory. They fought the Mongols for many years. Then, the Choson **dynasty** ruled Korea from 1392 to 1910.

Many different kingdoms ruled ancient Korea. Silla was an ancient Korean kingdom from 57 BC to AD 935. Monuments from this time can still be seen today.

In the early 1900s, Japan and Russia fought over Korea. After Japan won the war, it took control of the area. Japan ruled over Korea from 1910 to 1945. Koreans were forced to speak Japanese and take Japanese names.

World War II ended in 1945. The United States and Russia took over Korea. Korea separated into north and south areas. From 1950 to 1953, North and South Korea fought for control over the land.

Since the countries divided, South and North Korea have struggled to get along. In 2007, trains crossed the north-south border for the first time in 56 years.

President Kim Dae-Jung was the son of a farmer. He worked hard and became president in 1998. He served as president until 2003.

In 1953, an area 2.5 miles (4 km) wide was created between North and South Korea. It is a site for peace talks relating to the two countries.

TIMELINE

Around 3000 BC

Early Korean societies grew as many travelers came from what is now China. People created tools for fishing and farming.

1948

The **Republic** of Korea was established on August 15. Syngman Rhee became the first president. He won the next three elections in 1952, 1956, and 1960.

AD 1394

The city of Seoul was founded. Many new construction projects led to major growth in the city.

1950

Communist North Korea **invaded** South Korea. The Korean War ended after three years of fighting. More than 2.5 million people lost their lives. No peace agreement was ever reached.

1991

South Korea joined the United Nations. This organization helps keep peace around the world.

2013

In January, South Korea used a rocket to put a **satellite** in space. The satellite will collect facts about weather changes.

AN IMPORTANT SYMBOL

South Korea's flag was first created for Korea in 1882. After South Korea became its own country, it kept the same basic flag. The four sets of black bars stand for earth, water, fire, and heaven. The red and blue yin-yang **symbol** means balance between opposites.

South Korea's government is a **republic**. The country has nine **provinces**. The president is the head of state and commander of the armed forces. The prime minister is chosen by the president. And, the prime minister is second in command.

South Korea's flag is white. This color has been used in Korea throughout history to mean peace.

SAY IT

Park Geun-hye
PAHRK GUN-HYEH

In 2013, Park Geun-hye became South Korea's 11th president. The president serves a five-year term.

In 2015, Hwang Kyo-ahn became South Korea's prime minister. The prime minister may serve for life.

SAY IT

Hwang Kyo-ahn
WAHNG KEE-yoh-ahn

ACROSS THE LAND

South Korea has mountains, valleys, plains, and rivers. The Sobaek Mountains form a long *S* shape across the country. The highest peak of the Sobaek Mountains is 6,283 feet (1,915 m) high.

South Korea's weather changes with the seasons. One of the largest **monsoons** blows over southeastern Asia. It brings rain and heat to South Korea in the summer. In the winter, a monsoon blows in from the north and northwest. It brings cold, dry weather to the country.

SAY IT

Sobaek
soh-BAYK

Did You Know?

Seoul's average temperature in January is about 26°F (-3°C). The average temperature in August is about 78°F (25°C).

South Korea's Naktong River is 325 miles (523 km) long. It is the country's longest river. It runs to the Korea Strait.

Around 4,500 kinds of plants grow in South Korea. Oak, maple, and birch trees grow there.

People tearing down the forests and building houses have decreased many animal populations. Tigers, leopards, and bears have almost vanished in South Korea. Deer are still common in the country.

The area between North and South Korea has been mostly left alone since the Korean War. There are now many animals living in the open space between the countries.

The musk deer is a small deer found throughout South Korea. Males have long teeth that stick out of their mouths.

Earning a Living

South Korea is a hardworking country. Many people work in finance, business, or **tourism**. Others work in factories. They make goods such as cell phones, televisions, and computer parts.

South Korea is one of the world's major deep-sea fishing nations. People fish for mackerel, tuna, and salmon.

South Korean factories make goods that are sold across the globe. Many automobiles are made in the country.

LIFE IN SOUTH KOREA

South Korea has strong ties to its ancient ways of life. Many historic areas destroyed during the Korean War have been rebuilt.

Food is one way South Koreans keep their ancient social practices alive. Rice is a popular food in the country. People also eat fish, vegetables, and fruit.

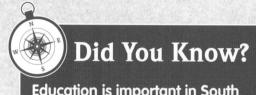

Did You Know?

Education is important in South Korea. The country has a high number of college students.

Kimchi is a spicy vegetable dish. It is one of the most popular foods in South Korea.

South Koreans value their country's music and dances. Some of the earliest Korean music came from tribes in northwestern Korea. These tribes combined singing and dancing as a way to practice their faith.

Early Koreans also used instruments to make music. A popular type of Korean drum is called the *changgo*. It has two sides that each make a different sound.

Faith is still important to many people in South Korea. People practice **Buddhism** and **Christianity**, among other beliefs.

Did You Know?

Tae kwon do and soccer are popular sports in South Korea.

SAY IT

changgo
CHAYN-goh

Many Korean dances honor people's faith and ways of life. Some dances include decorative fans and costumes.

Buddhist temples are often found in the mountains or other beautiful places. Many temples have Buddha statues, paintings, and bells.

FAMOUS FACES

Many talented people are from South Korea. Park Geun-hye was sworn in as South Korea's president in 2013. She was born on February 2, 1952, in the North Gyeongsang **province** of South Korea.

Park is the daughter of former President Park Chung Hee. She is a member of South Korea's Conservative Party. She aims for peace within South Korea.

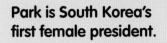
Park is South Korea's first female president.

31

Kim Yu-Na was a world-class figure skater. She was born on September 5, 1990, in the city of Bucheon. Kim began skating at age six.

Kim won a gold medal by taking first place at the 2010 Winter Olympics in Vancouver, Canada. In 2013, she won her second ISU World Figure Skating Championship. Kim **retired** from figure skating in 2014. Now, Kim is a spokesperson for many products in South Korea.

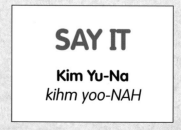

SAY IT

Kim Yu-Na
kihm yoo-NAH

Kim won the silver medal by taking second place at the 2014 Winter Olympics in Sochi, Russia.

TOUR BOOK

Imagine traveling to South Korea! Here are some places you could go and things you could do.

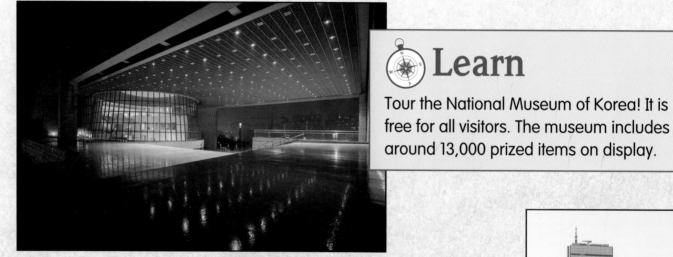

Learn

Tour the National Museum of Korea! It is free for all visitors. The museum includes around 13,000 prized items on display.

Climb

The 63 Building is a skyscraper in Seoul. When it opened in 1985, it was the tallest building in Asia!

Explore

Visit Olympic Park in Seoul, where the 1988 Summer Olympics were held. It has the country's largest sports center.

See

Visit the Pulguk Temple. This **Buddhist** temple was built in the mid-700s. It is known for its beautiful art.

Tour

See South Korea's Blue House in Seoul. It is home to the country's president.

A Great Country

The story of South Korea is important to our world. South Korea is a land of beautiful mountains and rivers. It is a country of talented and hardworking people.

The people and places that make up South Korea offer something special. They help make the world a more beautiful, interesting place.

Banpo Bridge is the world's longest bridge fountain. Water shoots off 3,740 feet (1,140 m) of this bridge.

SOUTH KOREA UP CLOSE

Official Name: Republic of Korea

Flag:

Population (rank): 49,115,196
(July 2015 est.)
(27th most-populated country)

Total Area (rank): 38,502 square miles
(109th largest country)

Capital: Seoul

Official Language: Korean

Currency: Won

Form of Government: Republic

National Anthem: "Aegukga"
(Patriotic Song)

IMPORTANT WORDS

Buddhism (BOO-dih-zuhm) a religion based in the teachings of Buddha.

capital a city where government leaders meet.

Christianity (krihs-chee-A-nuh-tee) a religion that follows the teachings of Jesus Christ.

Communist (KAHM-yuh-nihst) of or relating to a form of government in which all or most land and goods are owned by the state. They are then divided among the people based on need.

dynasty (DEYE-nuh-stee) a powerful group or family that rules for a long time.

electronics products that work by controlling the flow of electricity. These often do useful things.

invade to enter a place, such as a country, in order to take it over by force.

monsoon a seasonal wind in southern Asia that sometimes brings heavy rain.

province a large section within a country, like a state.

republic a government in which the people choose the leader.

retire to give up one's job.

satellite a man-made object meant to circle the earth, the moon, or something else in space.

symbol (SIHM-buhl) an object or mark that stands for an idea.

tourism the business of providing hotels, food, and activities for travelers.

World War II a war fought in Europe, Asia, and Africa from 1939 to 1945.

WEBSITES

To learn more about Explore the Countries, visit **booklinks.abdopublishing.com**. These links are routinely monitored and updated to provide the most current information available.

INDEX

animals **22, 23**
Asia **4, 20, 34**
Banpo Bridge **37**
Blue House **35**
Bucheon **32**
businesses **8, 10, 24, 25**
Dongdaemun Design Plaza **9**
East China Sea **6**
food **12, 26, 27**
government **15, 16, 18, 19, 30, 31, 35, 38**
Halla, Mount **5**
Hallasan National Park **5**
Hwang Kyo-ahn **19**
Inchon **10, 11**
Japan, Sea of **6**
Kim Dae-Jung **15**
Kim Yu-Na **32, 33**
Korea Strait **21**
language **4, 14, 38**

Naktong River **21**
National Museum of Korea **34**
natural resources **10, 24**
Park Chung Hee **30**
Park Geun-hye **19, 30, 31**
plants **22**
population **6, 8, 10, 38**
Pulguk Temple **35**
Pusan **10, 11**
Olympic Park **35**
religion **28, 29, 35**
Seoul **8, 9, 16, 20, 34, 35, 38**
63 Building **34**
size **6, 8, 38**
Sobaek Mountains **20**
sports **28, 32, 33, 35**
Syngman Rhee **16**
weather **17, 20**
Yellow Sea **6**